Interview with
BLACKBEARD
& Other Vicious Villains

Written by
Andy
Seed

Illustrated by
Gareth
Conway

WELBECK

Contents

Introduction

You know what? For this book, I could have interviewed anyone. Perhaps I should have had a little natter with some really NICE people. Like maybe a sweet old granny. Or that lady who runs the charity for wonky kittens. Or the kindly gent down the road who grows purple tulips in a window box and wears a tie 24/7.

But NO. Those people are nice but, well, maybe they are TOO NICE. Instead, I decided to interview BAD people. Villains. They are much more interesting - after all, these are the horrid humans from history who actually did all the REALLY MEAN things that the rest of us would never DARE to do because our mums would go so ballistic, they would BREAK THE WORLD.

So, yes, for this book I got to meet ten of the baddest baddies from back in time. I blathered to outrageous outlaws, ruthless gangsters, a potty emperor, two thieving pirates and a violent vampire (maybe). There was also a sneaky conman who sold the Eiffel Tower, and a man so TERRIBLE that his name was, well, Terrible! Yes, you can read my Q&A with all of them right here!

Ah, you want to know how I did it? OK, well, I am extremely lucky because I am one of the few authors around who has a TIME MACHINE that can also translate ancient languages and makes a decent cup of tea. Handy, eh? Yes, with my trusty tranimalator I can travel back to any year in history and still get home in time for pudding. Plus, it's very useful for getting me out of deathly-dangerous situations, as you'll see.

Sit back now, and enjoy the VILLAINOUS TRUTH...

Andy Seed

~ An interview with ~
Blackbeard

Well, I'm sailing in the sunny Caribbean in the year 1717, but this is NO CRUISE because the captain of this ship is the most FEARSOME PIRATE who ever lived... oh what have I DONE?

Q. Morning! First question: is Blackbeard your real name?
A. Arrr!

Q. Do you enjoy being a murderous pirate?
A. Arrrr!

Q. Do you always say, 'arrr'?
A. What? Oh, sorry. I was actually saying *arrghh* - I just dropped a cannonball on my toe.

Q. Ouch. Anyway, my question was: is Blackbeard your real name?
A. And who wants to know, exactly? You don't look like one of my crew. None of them dress that badly...

Q. Ah, yes, *I feared this might come up*... I am, er, looking for adventure.

A. Oh, so you want to join the crew? Have you had much buccaneering experience? Spent long at sea?

Q. Erm... yes... my pedalo once got tangled in seaweed near Rhyl. Anyway, *I'm* supposed to be asking the questions!

A. You do know I am the captain here, and this vessel is manned by a hundred cut-throats, don't you? Tell me, if you're a real sailor, what's this called?

Q. Erm, the mizzen? No, wait, it's the cringle!

A. It's the binnacle! The mizzen is a mast. Any true seaman would know that. What's the poop deck for?

Q. Well, I wouldn't like to say... sounds disgusting!

A. As I suspected, you're a spy. Probably a landlubber sent by the Navy to find my whereabouts. They've been after Blackbeard for years...

Q. But IS BLACKBIRD YOUR REAL NAME?

A. No, it's Black*beard*. Men, throw this troublemaker in the hold. We'll use him for bait when we meet some sharks, ha.

Q. What about Edward Teach?

A. WAIT! Leave him. Where did you hear that name? Who are you really?

Q. OK, time to tell the truth. My name is Andy and I'm from 200 years in the future and I've time-travelled here to interview you for a book. You're the one pirate everybody's heard of!

A. HAHAHAHA! Now THAT is a story! Well, spy or nay, you can certainly entertain the crew with crazy tales like that when we are out on the ocean.

Q. Perhaps you'll believe me if I tell you that you are from Bristol but became a privateer, running a boat out here in the West Indies, raiding Spanish ships for the British Government while the two countries were at war? You also lived on Jamaica for a time before visiting the Republic of Pirates in Nassau where you sailed with Benjamin Hornigold. True or not?

A. So, mysterious stranger, you know my story – well, a small part of it – perhaps I should believe you. Or maybe I should just save myself the trouble and throw you overboard. What do you want to know?

Q. I want to know how you became a pirate and what it's like, and if the stories about you in books are true. This is your chance to set the record straight, dispel the myths! Will you do it?

A. Well, why not. I can tell my story and still throw you into the sea if I feel like it... go ahead with your questions, Andrew of Tomorrowland.

Q. Ah, thank you, finally. Right, so why did you become a pirate?

A. Why indeed... it's a dishonest and dangerous life but an exciting one. It beats sitting behind a desk in some dusty town... Like you said, ten years ago I was out here in the Caribbean, commanding a fast, well-armed sloop and capturing Spanish treasures from ships sailing from their colonies. I loved the life of a privateer, and I had the blessing of good Queen Anne too.

Q. Oh right, you mean you captured boats going from America to Spain - so what was the treasure? Gold and jewels?

A. Occasionally gold, often silver. But there are other kinds of treasure out here in the West Indies: sugar, wine, rum, cocoa, cotton, indigo dye - they are worth good money.

Q. So, you were a kind of legalised pirate because England was at war with Spain and France, fighting over who would control Europe and which colonies in America would belong to which country?

A. It was a bit more complicated than that, but yes. Then the war ended in 1713 and I was out here. I didn't want to go back and live in Jamaica or cold, damp Britain. I enjoyed the life at sea, I was a good sailor and the men trusted me. Besides, we had guns and cannon and the Spanish merchant ships were still loaded with rich cargoes...

Q. You carried on robbing them then?

A. Well, not at first. I thought about becoming a slave trader but then I heard about this island in the Bahamas controlled by pirates. There were stories about it everywhere. The Republic of Pirates. I had to go and see for myself.

Q. What was it like?

A. Lawless, rough, treacherous... There was too much chance of having your throat slit in a place like that. Instead, I joined the crew of a crafty skipper, Ben Hornigold. We soon captured some vessels and he gave one to me to command. We sailed together and plundered Spanish goods.

Q. **What did you do with the captured ships? Jump aboard and murder the crew?**

A. Ah, so you don't know everything... No, my lad, that is not my way. I split from Hornigold after a while. My men said we should loot *every* ship, even the British. By this time, I had a bigger craft with more guns, the *Revenge*. I led a bold crew, with three boats in all. And I learned there was no need for bloodshed.

Q. **How? What? I thought you were a vicious, evil brute?**

A. Ha, then you are mistaken! I am a big man but I also wore imposing clothes, a tall hat and I grew my dark beard long and had it plaited. We flew black flags with death heads in them. I looked like a terror, a fearsome sight, and that was enough...

Q. **What do you mean?**

A. When sailors on captured ships saw me, they said I was a devil! They were convinced I was going to kill them all, especially as I always wore six pistols. So they just handed over their cargoes without a fight. Easy! Especially when I added a bit of fire...

Q. Fire?

A. Yes, I tucked some lit fuses into my hat where they hung down, spitting sparks and smoke. That really convinced them I was more demon than man. But I never killed anyone.

Q. And did you ever say, 'Me hearties'?

A. No.

Q. 'Shiver me timbers'?

A. Eh?

Q. I won't mention 'pieces of eight'.

A. Good. What else do you want to know?

Q. Why are you so secretive about your real name?

A. You may think I'm just a filthy pirate robber, but I am an educated man from a good family. I want to protect them in case I am captured. I don't want them to be blamed for my misdeeds.

Q. So, you know what you are doing is wrong?

A. Of course! It's stealing. But where did this treasure come from? The Spanish have looted the American lands to the south for centuries. They invaded and just took whatever they wanted from the local people. The British and French did the same. And they put slaves to work all over these islands in the West Indies, growing sugar. They grew rich from all of that. So I have taken some of their ill-gotten wealth.

Q. Right, I see. This ship must be full of money. Are you going to bury it?
A. What, bury a ship? That would be a BIG hole...

Q. No, I mean... oh never mind, I know you're going to tell me pirates don't bury treasure, so I won't ask. What ship is this, by the way?
A. The *Queen Anne's Revenge*. I captured it from the French and added 40 cannons. Of course, our dear queen is dead now and we have some German called George on the throne. PAH.

Q. So, what are your plans next?
A. As you can see, I now have several vessels at my command, enough to blockade a port in the colonies.

Q. What does that mean?
A. We're heading for South Carolina, on the American coast. There's a town there called Charleston. My ships are going to block the harbour and rob anyone sailing in or out. Easy pickings. But what I really want are medicines.

Q. Are you ill? Fuse burns, maybe? Scurvy? Wooden leg rash?

A. As you can see, my legs are flesh and bone, strange man. No, pirate crew are not, well, the *healthiest* of human beings... In fact - they stink. And when we call into ports they're always catching diseases from the locals. I need a fit crew, not a bunch of sickly idlers!

Q. What if there are soldiers at Charleston, or the Royal Navy arrive?

A. Then we will fight them! We have a LOT of firepower. But I have heard that the king wants to send a fleet of warships here to stop we pirates from wrecking trade in the Caribbean. If that happens, I may take the Royal Pardon.

Q. Pardon?

A. I may take... Oh, haha, a joke. Of sorts. No, it means the king will let us go unpunished if we give up our piracy. I hear Ben Hornigold has already gone that way...

Q. Right, that's all my questions answered. Thank you, Blackbeard! Or should I say, Mr Teach...

A. Men, THROW HIM OVERBOARD NOW!

Q. Go tranimalator, GO!

Blackbeard bashed

What happened next?

- Blackbeard and his pirate ships did blockade Charleston in 1718.
- The Governor of Virginia then hired some Royal Navy ships and sailors to ambush Blackbeard.
- There was a battle on the American coast and Blackbeard's men were outnumbered.
- He died after taking five gunshots and 20 sword cuts.
- His head was cut off and placed at the front of a Navy ship as a warning to other pirates.

The real end of pirates of the Caribbean

The Royal Navy sailed with a powerful fleet of ships and destroyed the Republic of Pirates in the Bahamas. They protected merchant ships and so put an end to pirates like Blackbeard who had terrorised the West Indies for decades.

A shipwreck rises

In 1996, the wreck of Blackbeard's ship the *Queen Anne's Revenge* was found on the seabed near the US coast. Over 300,000 items have been recovered from the wreck including:

- 31 cannons and 400 cannonballs
- The ship's anchor ● Coins
- Weapons ● But no treasure.

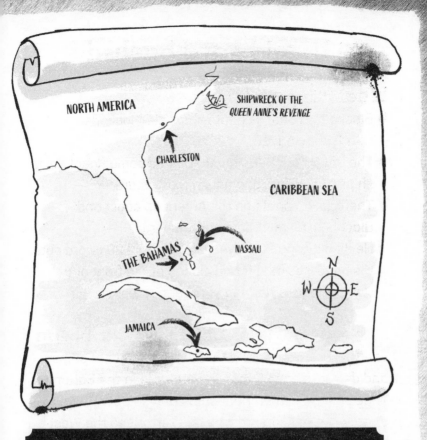

NORTH AMERICA

SHIPWRECK OF THE
QUEEN ANNE'S REVENGE

CHARLESTON

CARIBBEAN SEA

THE BAHAMAS

NASSAU

JAMAICA

FACTbeard

- Blackbeard was an active pirate for only about two years.
- There is no evidence he killed anyone, despite his reputation.
- His real name WAS Edward Teach.
- No one knows for sure where he came from or lived – his secrets died with him.

An interview with

Guy Fawkes

I'm now in London in the year 1605. Well, I think I am - it's SO DARK in here I can hardly see a thing. I'm in some kind of big, gloomy cellar, hoping to speak to someone very well-known indeed...

Q. Is there anybody there?
A. No.

Q. OK, I'll be going then... WAIT! If you spoke, you must be there. Who are you?
A. No one, it's just your imagination. Go away.

Q. Hang on, this is hopeless, I can't see ANYTHING - I need some light.
A. STOP! Do not strike a match, I beg you! I will talk. Here, I have a small lamp.

Q. Ah, that's better, thanks. Oof, it's really cold and damp in here. Er, why are you sitting in a dark cellar and what is your name?

A. I am a fuel merchant – I supply wood and coal – look, here are my stores.

Q. But why were you sitting in the dark? And why were you so scared that I would light a match?

A. You have many questions. Perhaps I should ask YOU what you are doing here? This is private property.

But anyway, I'm here to guard this fuel for my master, Thomas Percy and I don't want it to, er, go up in flames, do I? I'm low on lamp oil too. Now, be on your way, please, good sir.

Q. **But you haven't told me your name. Who are you?**
A. I am John Johnson.

Q. **John Johnson?** *John Johnson!* **That sounds like a MADE-UP name to me. Are you sure you aren't Tom Thompson or Ben Benson? How about Maximillian Maximillianson?**
A. Stranger, you are testing my patience. I have a sharp axe here... Be gone!

Q. **What if I asked you if you were... GUY FAWKES?**
A. How do you know that name? Who are you? Who sent you? Is this some kind of trick, or a test? Or maybe you are one of the palace guards? You don't look like a man of arms to me.

Q. **Whoah, stop! So many questions. Look, I'm not one of your enemies, and I'm not going to give you away, I promise. In fact, I know why you're here underneath the Houses of Parliament. I even know what's in the barrels you have hidden behind this pile of wood. If I said, '*boom*', would that convince you?**
A. But, how do you know this? Are you a friend of Catesby, or Wintour?

Q. No I'm not. It's kind of, well, tricky to explain. But if you just answer my questions, I promise I won't tell ANYONE you're here. (*Well, apart from several thousand kids in about 420 years' time...*) Er, is that a deal?

A. Very well, you don't seem dangerous. More kind of unhinged. But be quick.

Q. Right, so, what was your childhood like?

A. I was a happy lad in the early days. We lived in the great city of York and my father had a good job along with a little property too. But then he died when I was eight. They were troubled times after that...

Q. What happened?

A. Hmmm, I may as well tell you, as you seem to know all about me anyway. My mother was a Catholic and she married again, into a Catholic family. Since it is outlawed for us to hold church services, we had to do things in secret. We risked our lives hiding priests and more.

Q. What about when you grew up?

A. My new family sent me to a good school and there I met other Catholics. They whispered about powerful men who shared our faith and who had plans to overthrow the queen and restore England to the true church. But nothing ever happened to change things.

Q. But how did you end up here, in London? Did you come sightseeing and get lost?

A. It is indeed a long story... I decided I had had enough of this wicked country. When I was old enough, I sold all I had and went to Spain.

Q. Ah, a nice holiday? A bit of sun and beach? Did you get a cheap galleon ticket?

A. Stop jabbering, man! I went there because it is a Catholic country! I wanted to help them fight their holy war against the Dutch Protestants. I became a soldier.

Q. So what brought you back? You don't seem to, erm, like this country very much.

A. I do what I believe is right. When Queen Elizabeth died and King James came down from Scotland to take the throne, I heard about a plan to destroy him and restore a Catholic monarchy. I returned to England and joined the leaders of this plot.

Q. Ah, was that Robert Catesby and the other geezer you mentioned?

A. Thomas Wintour, yes. There were others too, good Catholic gentlemen who decided to act.

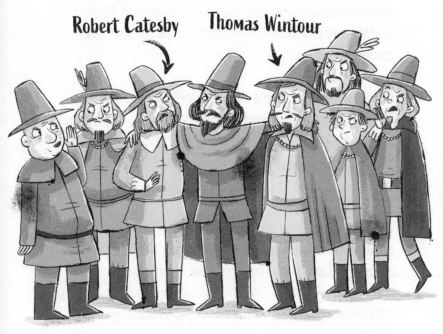

Robert Catesby   Thomas Wintour

Q. Gentlemen? It doesn't sound very gentle to blow up the king and the Houses of Parliament!

A. That is true. But these are drastic times. The rulers of this country have made our lives a misery and so we must obliterate them. I am to light the fuse, being the only one who understands how to handle explosives. Tomorrow, at the State Opening of Parliament, the king and all of those who run this wretched nation will die.

Q. Isn't that, well, just a teeny bit, MURDERY?

A. That is not a proper word. But anyway, we believe that they are defying God himself. Perhaps that's why we have been able to smuggle 36 barrels of gunpowder unseen, here, into these rooms right underneath the building where Parliament meets tomorrow.

Q. Are you not worried someone will find out?

A. How could they find out? I have been here for weeks and no one has searched the place. The other plotters are over a hundred miles away! Success is ours.

Q. Well, just SUPPOSE one of your gang had, say, a close Catholic friend who was a member of the House of Lords and who would die in the blast tomorrow. And SUPPOSE they warned him, with SAY, a letter... and he showed that letter to... THE KING?

A. I know of no such letter! Strange man, I feel you know something more. What are you hiding from me? Now, where's that axe?

Q. Do you know what, I think it may be TIME TO GO! I promise I'll remember remember you...

A. What? Eh? Come back!

Guy Talks

What happened next?

- There was indeed a mysterious unsigned letter warning a lord to stay away the next day.
- King James I ordered the buildings to be searched – Fawkes was arrested and the gunpowder found.
- Fawkes was tortured in the Tower of London, to force him to reveal the names of the other plotters.
- They were rounded up, found guilty of High Treason, and executed in a grisly way as a warning to other plotters.

Houses of Parliament

The Gunpowder Plot

How is this moment in history still remembered each November 5th in Britain?

- People celebrate that the plot was stopped – traditionally by having a bonfire.
- Fireworks have been lit on bonfire night for over 350 years.
- Some people also burn a dummy on the fire, called a guy.
- People often gather round the fire to eat special foods and watch fireworks.

That REALLY hurts

Torturing prisoners was not a nice business at all:

- At first, Fawkes was questioned by the king but would not say who else was in the plot
- The king then gave permission for Fawkes to be sent for torture in the Tower of London.
- He held out for three days but revealed names after he was put on the rack.
- The rack was a cruel, painful device that stretched the victim, pulling their joints apart.

Nero

It's the year 66 and I am in the greatest city on Earth, that's Rome, to have a little chat with one of its naughtiest emperors to see what he has to say. OH YES!

Q. Hail Nero! How's it going?
A. Who are YOU?

Q. I'm, well, a traveller who has a few questions, that's all. May I ask them?
A. Be GONE, bearded oik! I am Emperor of Rome, I have no time for such trivialities...

Q. Wait! Actually I am from the future – I wander through time itself.
A. The future? OOOH! What's it like? Have a seat, tell me everything.

Q. Ah, thanks. Right, so, the future is, well, kind of *different*. We spend a lot of time staring at this big flat thing called a TV.

A. Why?

Q. Good question. Most things on it are TOTAL GARBAGE. But that's not all we do. We stare at other flat things too, computers and phones. Does this make any sense?

A. No, none. I am confused as to why there is so much staring. What else do you do?

Q. Queuing mainly. But can we talk about your life?

A. The future sounds DISMAL. Hopefully the Roman Empire is still in charge, though?

Q. Er, no.

A. WHAT! Perhaps you lie? How do I know you are telling the truth? The future cannot be that bad.

Q. Oh, wait, I know. Look, here's my phone. I'll take a selfie of us. Come on, SMILE!

A. What's going on? OOOH, is that me? That is AMAZING! Truly supernatural. I understand now... you are not just a man, you are a GOD, kind of like me! Only someone immortal can perform such sorcery! What is your name, O Divine One?

Q. Andy... No wait. *This could be rather useful... What kind of thing do they call their gods? Oh yes, planets - Jupiter, Venus, Mercury and all that. But all the good ones are taken... Oh, I know...* **Ahem, yes my name is Asteroid.**

A. Nice! I am honoured by your visit, Android. Please have some grapes.

Q. I have questions for you first, Nero. How did you become Emperor?

A. Ah well, it used to be Claudius, my stepdad, but he had an unfortunate meeting with Death, so I became the big E. I was only 17 as well.

Q. Some say that your mother Agrippina, Claudius's wife, killed him with poison so her son - you - would become ruler. Is that true?

A. Nonsense! He was old and he ate and drank too much. I think he just... popped.

Q. Your mother is dead now too, isn't she?

A. Well, yes, a bit.

Q. Very dead, I think. And the history books of the future say you killed her! How could you kill your own mum? If I did that to my mum she'd be FURIOUS.

A. Look, can't we talk about the good things I've done? I mean, I was a really popular Emperor at first. I held lots of games and celebrations - the ordinary people of Rome loved me!

Q. But what about the nobles, and the men who run the city, the Senate? They thought you were just a showman who didn't really care about running the Roman Empire or even know how to do it.

A. Well, it's just SO STUPIDLY BIG. How could I possibly govern all of this land plus most of Europe, parts of Asia and Africa and that unruly island Britannica where Boudica has just been revolting as well? It's TOO HARD.

Q. Ah, Britain, that's where I am from! Have you been there? I recommend the fish and chips in Bridlington.

A. Eh? I thought you gods lived in the heavens on Mount Olympus?

Q. Er, yes, yes, indeed – me and Mars and the rest. I love a nice snowy peak. Anyway, why *did* you do your mother in?

A. She wouldn't let me marry the gorgeous Poppaea! It just wasn't FAIR. And she kept telling me how to run the Empire, so I got rid of her and those other advisers she appointed.

Q. I see. At least you're married to Poppaea now, aren't you?

A. No, she's dead. I accidentally kicked her too hard.

Q. A lot of people seem to die around you... Anyway, are you a popular leader now?

A. Huh, NO I AM NOT. And that's not fair either. People still think I started the Great Fire of Rome. I mean, COME ON, why would I burn down half of my own city?

Q. Maybe to clear the land so you can build an ENORMOUS and hugely expensive new palace called the Golden House? All the people who lost their homes in the blaze don't like that at all, do they?

A. Well, I need performing space for my poetry, singing and acting! I need to practise playing the lyre too - I'm doing a MEGA-TOUR of Greece and entering all of the talent contests soon. I can't wait!

Q. But I read that the Senators and other important people in Rome think it's all a waste of time and money. They think you should be visiting your Empire abroad and fighting wars and winning victories like the other Emperors did. That's what the people love, isn't it?

A. Ugh. I don't CARE. I'm not interested in fighting and battles. If we conquer more lands the empire will be EVEN BIGGER and harder to run. I like poems, not killing people.

Q. Then why have you just fed the Christians of Rome to lions?

A. I had to blame *someone* for the fire...

Q. Do you feel you've gone from Nero the hero to Nero the zero?

A. Here, have some of these grapes – they're not poisoned, I promise...

Oh, wait a sec, I left some veggie nuggets in the oven. Must dash.

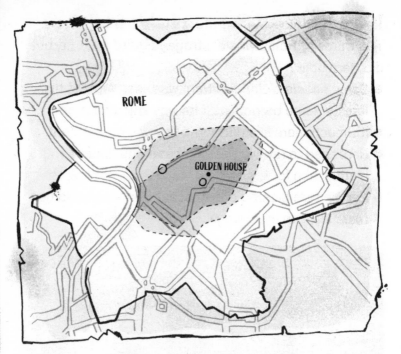

Nero oh dear-o

What happened next?

- Nero spent a whole year in Greece performing plays, poems, songs and music.
- He won 1,800 prizes in the festivals he took part in - that's all of them!
- But in Rome, the people and the senators turned against him.
- He ran away from the city and killed himself, knowing he was doomed.

Was the Great Fire really his fault?

Two thirds of Rome was destroyed by fire in 64 CE, but did Nero do it?

- Some people claim that Nero was seen playing his lyre as Rome burned, as if he was enjoying it.
- It's much more likely that the fire was an accident.
- Nero tried to rebuild the city, but many people blamed him for the fire.
- Nero in turn blamed the innocent Christians and had them killed in cruel ways.

Nasty Nero
What else did he do?
- He had his first wife executed.
- He had prisoners set on fire.
- He made people pay heavy taxes to fund his extravagant giant palace.
- He paid people to clap at his singing shows.

An interview with
Ned Kelly

And now a natter in 1879 with possibly the number one AUSSIE outlaw of all time, a legendary name down under. But some say he wasn't a villain at all! Let's find out, shall we...

Q. Can we talk, Mr Nelly, I mean Mr Kelly?

A. WHATTT! WHO THE BLAZES ARE YOU? Where did you come from? And what is that pile of JUNK next to you?

Q. Oi! That's my tranimalator - it's a time machine. I'm from the future and I'd like to interview you. Is that OK?

A. You gave me a right fright, fella, just appearing like that. From the future, you say? Haha, I meet some right wackos out here in the bush. Not used to the hot sun, eh, mate? Made yer nut go a bit doolally, has it?

Q. *Right, I hoped honesty would work but...* **Alright Ned, mate, I was just kiddin ya, haha. I'm, er, a bushranger like you, on the run from the law. But listen, I know people who work for publishers. If you tell me your story, I'll get them to print the truth, instead of all the made-up rubbish people keep writing about your gang.**

A. Oh right, that's different then. Yeah, in fact that would be BONZA. I've been trying to give my version of events for years. The police and the newspapers and politicians spread lies about me all the time. It's an INJUSTICE! -

Q. So where are the rest of the Kelly Gang?

A. Oh, my brother Dan's gone off to get some tucker from a friend, and Joe and Steve are just east, watching one of the search parties that's trying to find us. There's an 8,000-dollar reward for our arrest, you know.

Q. Wow, in our money that's about... A LOT. Definitely over half a million. But why are you wanted?

A. *Your* money? Isn't there only one kind in Australia? Anyway, we're wanted for robbery and murder. The authorities have declared us outlaws. But the truth is, we're innocent.

Q. What does that actually mean, 'outlaws'.

A. I tell you what it means, mate. It means anyone can just SHOOT US DEAD and face no charges!

Q. Ouch, that sounds painful. I hope they don't think I'm one of your gang... *I knew I should have bought those bulletproof undies at the market.* But anyway, how did it all start?

A. It started with my dad. He was transported here from Ireland on a convict ship for stealing two pigs.

Q. Two pigs? Are you telling porkies? Sorry. Is that true?

A. Yeah, course it's true. This is a colony of the rotten British Empire, ain't it? They've been dumping 'undesirable' people here for a hundred years. So, after his sentence they told him to farm some patch of rocky dry desert. Impossible. He had a family, including me – how were we supposed to survive?

Q. I've no idea. It is VERY hot and dry here. So what happened?

A. He turned to drink and died when I was twelve. We were a family of squatters with no hope, so I got involved with a few bad fellas – bushrangers. They stole horses mainly. But we were poor and hungry. Life was hell for my old ma.

Q. So you got into crime?

A. You call it crime, I call it survival. The poor of Australia like us are treated like DIRT by the authorities. They don't care. Because my dad was a convict, they treated us all like convicts, even the kids...

Q. I can see you're angry... Did you try to get a job when you were a bit older? You look like a big strong guy, Ned.

A. Sure, I did all sorts of work. But I still ended up in jail when I was fifteen. I got blamed for a crime I didn't do. Two and a half years in a prison full of hard, brutal men... I was just a kid! Can you see why I hate the law?

Q. I'm fairly sure I can. So how did you end up with your own gang, hiding out here in the bush, miles from any towns?

A. It started last year really. An officer came to our house to arrest me for stock theft. He had hold of my brother Dan when I arrived there. I couldn't bear for Dan to go to jail, so I fired a shot and injured the man and we got away. We were wanted after that – we had to hide out here.

Q. You mentioned murder earlier. Did the policeman die?

A. No, it was just a little wound! The problem was that we had to rob banks to get money to survive. My old mates Joe and Steve joined us but a troop of four police with guns tracked us down to Stringybark Creek and there was a shootout. They were trying to kill us. We shot and killed three of them in self-defence. That's when they declared us outlaws.

Q. I get it. That's serious. How have you managed to survive out here in the wild for so long?

A. We know this country. We were brought up here, and we're tough, we're survivors. And there's plenty of friends who help us because they know we've been wronged. The police won't leave my family alone – and the other poor families here in Victoria.

Q. Is it true you called the police 'ugly, fat-necked, wombat-headed and big bellied'?

A. Yes, because THEY ARE. I wrote a letter to them saying so. The devils sent my mother to jail for THREE YEARS HARD LABOUR. And she has a baby too.

Q. Did you say you wrote a LETTER? To the POLICE? Why?

A. Sure, I wrote two. The second one was 56 pages long: I had a LOT to say. I wanted it printed in the newspapers so everyone would know what really happened. Instead they made me sound like a cold-blooded madman. But it's alright now because you're going to tell it right, aren't you, mate? Because if you didn't...

Q. *Gulp.* Yes, sure, I promise this interview will be printed, er, in the future. So, erm, what else was in that BEAST of a letter?

A. I told the police to leave us squatter families alone or face terrible consequences.

Q. You threatened the POLICE? Won't that just make them MORE ANGRY? They'll come after you even harder, surely? I heard they are bringing in soldiers with more guns.

A. Maybe. But I want people to know about Ned Kelly's mistreatment. Anyway, we aren't scared of the law's guns. We've got PROTECTION!

Q. Have you? What kind? A tank? Guided missiles? Or maybe you bought those bullet-proof undies at the market?

A. I didn't understand a word of that, fella. No, we got ARMOUR. Look - we made it ourselves from thick plough metal. Shots just bounce off it: we tested!

Q. You're going to WEAR that? In a GUN BATTLE with police and soldiers? It must weigh a ton! And you'll look like, well, pound shop medieval knights.

A. We survived for years without it; with it we'll be invincible. Now fella it's time to say g'day. I need to wet some sand, if you get my meaning.

Q. Thanks Ned, and erm, good luck.

A. Give me a good write up, or I'll DO YA.

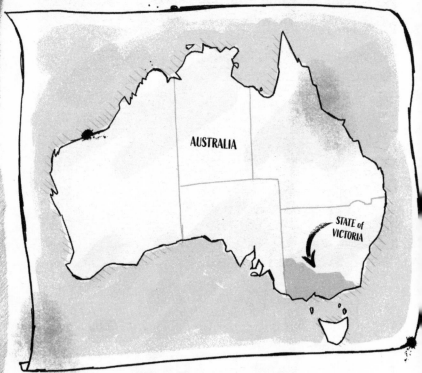

Ned no more

What happened next?

- The Kelly Gang were tracked down by armed police. They took hostages into a small hotel.
- There was a big gun battle, with the gang wearing their armour.
- Ned was badly wounded in the hand and legs, the other three were killed.
- Ned Kelly was captured and hanged for murder on 11th November 1880.

Hero or villain?

Ned Kelly really divides opinion in Australia - what do you think?

- Some say he and his family were victims, never given fair treatment.
- Others say he was a brutal, murderous criminal.
- Some say he tried to help the poor stand up against the cruel authorities, like Robin Hood.
- Others say not everyone turned to crime, and Kelly got what he deserved.

Grisly reminders

These are all on display in Australia today:

- The ramshackle remains of the tin shack that was Kelly's childhood home.
- The epic rambling letter he wrote to the police and others.
- The armour he wore, complete with 18 bullet marks.
- His death mask (a plaster cast of his face made after execution).

~ An interview with ~

Ivan the Terrible

It's all very well having a TIME MACHINE that can whizz you through the past, but if it lands you right in front of one of history's most dreaded tyrants then it's NOT so much fun. Here I am in 1582 in Russia in just that situation... Eek!

Q. Is it OK if we chat, Mister, er, Terrible?
A. EURRRAARRGGHH!

Q. What's up? Have I left blobs of yoghurt on my face again?
A. A g-g-ghost! Do not harm me, strange spirit, I beg.

Q. Whoops, sorry. I know I just suddenly appeared, but I'm not here to haunt you, honest. I'm just, well, mysteriously appearing in the name of research.
A. Not a ghoul, you say? But you are pale and sinister...

Q. Yeah, that's what my friends say too. Though I prefer pale and interesting.

A. Wait, I know who you are! I have been praying for months for someone who can bear to hear the truth of my past. I need to confess my dark deeds. You must be the one.

Q. Well, OK, that's sort of what I'm here for - to see what you have to say. But isn't *that* kind of confessing usually done, you know, in a church?

A. Indeed. But the priests are terrified of me. And I've robbed most of the bishops and taken the treasures from their cathedrals. I even made the Archbishop of Novgorod marry a HORSE.

Don't forget the ring!

Q. Ah, I can see why they might not be so enthusiastic about meeting you... But I'm ready to hear everything, if that's OK?

A. Yes, yes, I need to admit what I have done, to tell of how many souls I have destroyed. I am tortured by guilt ever since I killed my own son.

Q. Oh dear, not good. What happened?

A. It was an accident, I swear, a fit of rage... I thought he was opposing me... I should not have struck him with an iron bar. And now he is dead I have no heir to become the next Tsar of Russia...

Q. No more children?

A. Well, I have a younger son, Fyodor, but he will make a shabby ruler. He's CLUELESS.

Q. Can I ask you something?

A. What?

Q. Are you really terrible or just quite bad?

A. Eh?

Q. Well, your name is Ivan the Terrible so...

A. What are you talking about? No one calls me that. Although I could understand it. The word really means 'FEARSOME' anyway, not BAD. But I can understand why people use that... I have struck much fear into many...

Q. When did it all start?

A. A good question! In a way I was doomed from the beginning - my destiny to be the ruler of such a vast, troubled land was always going to lead to bloodshed. Did you know I was made Grand Prince of Moscow at age THREE?

Q. Yikes, I bet your toddler tantrums were SPECTACULAR. But why so young? It must be quite hard to be in charge of a country when you're still potty training?

A. Indeed. It was because my father died. I also lost my mother when I was eight. So there I was, an orphan crowded round with scheming 'advisers' who wanted power. But I showed them I was capable - I became Tsar of Russia at just 16!

Q. So when did the, er, *trouble* begin?

A. Things went well at first. I expanded the empire
– I marched south with an army and conquered
troublesome places like Kazan. The people loved
that. I also clamped down on crime, putting an end
to bandits and dishonest tax collectors.

Q. You don't sound too terrible to me! What else
happened?

A. If you were a ruler you'd understand how hard it can
be. Everybody wants you to make their lives better,
but you cannot please everybody. I had trouble with
the nobles – the powerful rich families who owned
the land across Russia.

Q. What kind of trouble?

A. They did not like my new laws. They thought I was taking away their local control of their territories. They plotted against me. I was sure the church was involved too... I had to stop them.

Q. Oh right, I see where this is going... What did you do?

A. I created a kind of large private army to seek out troublemakers. They wore black robes. I let them loose against the nobles and their supporters. It is hard for me to admit, but I went too far...

Q. I read about this in books. Your thugs killed a lot of people, didn't they?

A. Thousands. Thousands more were tortured. Most were innocent, I fear. Those brutal soldiers of mine were cruel because I was cruel. Rich and poor were burned. Women and children were thrown into icy rivers to drown. Others starved. It was a massacre against my own people...

Q. So why did you do it, so much evil? You must have known it was wrong, surely?

A. But at the time I thought I was doing the work of God, truly. I believed he had appointed me, so I had a divine duty to bring the torments of hell to those who opposed me.

Q. And what do you think now?

A. Now? My son is gone. My wife is dead. The people hate me. I ruled in rage because I felt I had to control everything. I was wrong. To think that you can just wipe out anyone who disagrees with you? Wrong. WRONG. When you called me terrible, you were right.

Wow! Well, I didn't expect THAT. I must go now, so, erm, thank you and I hope you soon become Ivan the Nice. See you later!

A terrible end

What happened next?

- Ivan became more and more unwell in the 1580s.
- The more people he killed, the more enemies he faced.
- In 1584, after playing a game of chess he fell over and dropped dead.
- Ivan was correct that his son Fyodor would not be a successful Tsar.

MOSCOW

RUSSIA

RUSSIA IN IVAN'S DAY WAS A LOT SMALLER THAN IT IS NOW.

Some more terrible things

Ivan was NOT the kind of person to upset...

- He threw dogs and cats off balconies.
- He had more wives than Henry VIII – probably seven (but no one is sure!).
- As well as killing his son, he probably disposed of other people in his family.
- His gang of soldiers on horseback robbed whoever they liked.

Did he do ANYTHING good?

Even villains and terrible rulers occasionally have better days:

- He built the magnificent St Basil's Cathedral, Moscow's most famous building.
- He did reduce some kinds of crime in Russia.
- He improved trade with countries such as England.
- He brought printed books to Russia for the first time.

~ An interview with ~

Victor Lustig

I now find myself inside a famous prison on a small island near San Francisco. It's the year 1946 and I'm with one of the world's greatest (or worst) ever SWINDLERS. Let's find out what he did...

Q. How are you liking Alcatraz, Mr Lustig?
A. It's a jail. It's cold, unhealthy, boring and harsh. What did you expect, dear fellow?

Q. It's also probably the most famous prison in the world, built on this small rocky island surrounded by dangerous ocean currents. Why did they bring you *here*?

A. Ah yes, good question. Well, you see, I'm good at evading the law. I've had the cops and government agents chasing me across America for decades. Now they've finally got me, they certainly don't want me to escape again...

Q. Again?

A. Indeed. I escaped from a jail in New York just before my trial. I faked illness and made a rope by tying torn strips of bed sheets together. I climbed out of the window and ran away. It was rather a lark!

Q. So how long have you been in this jail?

A. Ten years. Ten miserable years... what a waste of a man's life... They say Alcatraz is escape-proof but I shall keep trying.

Q. So, what exactly was your offence? No wait, tell me your story - how did you get into crime in the first place?

A. Why not? I've nothing else to do, hey old chap... Well, I was born in a small village in Europe, in

Austria-Hungary as it was known then. I was a clever boy, too clever really, always getting into trouble for my cheek. As soon as I was old enough I went to Paris. I had no money so survived by picking pockets, cheating at gambling, doing card tricks and so on. I was good at it.

Q. So, how did you end up here, across the other side of the world nearly?

A. It's quite a tale... In Paris I was a young, handsome and clever man, but I wasn't rich and that's what I wanted. I was too lazy to work so I decided to trick my way to wealth. And I did it!

Q. Wow. How?

A. I watched rich people. Some of them were smart but many weren't. I worked out how to *relieve* them of a portion of their cash. They could afford it. I dressed well, used my charm and my many languages. It worked best on ocean liners at first.

Q. What, you mean the big passenger ships sailing to and from America?

A. Exactly. Full of First Class victims, haha. I told them I was a successful musical producer who was planning a big Broadway show in New York. I convinced them it was going to be a huge hit and could make a LOT of money for them, but I needed investment.

Q. So they just gave you their money?

A. Well, old fellow, it's not as easy as that... I won them over, got their confidence by spending time with them and appearing to be a charming, reliable, likeable chap you see.

Q. Ah right, you're a confidence trickster - a con man?

A. I find that phrase vulgar but yes, it's true. I swindled the silly fools out of thousands...

Q. But didn't anyone check up on you, see if you were who you said you were? I would just Google you and know in a flash!

A. Goggle me? What's that? This was the 1910s. They were on a ship at sea - there was no way to check anything!

Q. No one had a phone?

A. A telephone? AT SEA! Don't be ridiculous, the cable would snap.

Q. Right, the past is a bit different, I forgot for a moment there... So did you do other scams too?

A. Hundreds! Once I had success, I couldn't stop. My personal favourite was back in elegant Paris. I sold the Eiffel Tower to some twit.

Q. What? WHAT! Did I just hear right? You SOLD THE EIFFEL TOWER?

A. Yes. Twice.

Q. YOU HAVE GOT TO BE KIDDING ME. HOW? You didn't *own* it, did you?

A. Of course not! I read in the newspapers that the French government were finding it too expensive to repair the tower and paint it. It was looking shabby. A lot of people thought it should be pulled down to save the cost.

Q. Pull down the Eiffel Tower? Buffoons! Anyway, how did you get involved?

A. I saw an opportunity. I met a forger and got him to make me some fake 'official' government notepaper. I posed as a senior Ministry officer in charge of the tower and I wrote to several of the biggest scrap metal dealers in Paris, ha.

Q. What did the letter say?

A. I told them that this was highly secret, but the Eiffel Tower was to be dismantled and sold for scrap. They could make a bid to buy the iron as long as they told no one.

Q. Sneaky! So you just took their money?

A. No, no. Things in the real world are rarely so simple! You would never make a hustler, I can see. Anyway, I found out which of the scrap men was most desperate to win the contract. I spoke to him and said if he offered me a *bribe* – a huge payment – I would make sure the tower was his. The silly mark fell for it. He gave me a fortune in cash, haha!

Q. He was called Mark? Doesn't sound French to me...

A. No, that's what we call the person who falls for the con – the mark. The secret is to spot the right one, the easy victim, the gullible guy – or lady. But you have to charm them, make them BELIEVE in you.

Q. And did you do the same trick again?

A. Yes! With another group of scrap merchants, although someone rather spoiled it by telling the police...

Q. What other scams did you do?

A. Ha, so many, so many. I think my favourite was the *Rumanian Box*.

Q. What the heck was that?

A. In America I made this smart wooden box with levers and dials on it. I told people it could copy any bank note in the world. I showed them how it could make a copy of a ten-dollar bill on plain paper – but I had a real one hidden in the machine to fool them, you see. I sold the box LOADS of times – even to a sheriff in Texas once!

Q. A policeman? WHAAAAT!

A. Quite true. He chased me across the States. Unfortunately, the law were really onto me by then so I changed schemes and got into forging money. I met Bill Watts, the best forger in the US. Together we printed these counterfeit hundred-dollar bills. They were works of ART.

Q. But didn't people spot it was fake money?

A. Not at first. It was so good it even fooled the banks. We made millions, literally!

Q. But you got caught in the end?

A. Alas, yes. It was too easy - federal agents tracked us down. The judge sentenced me to 20 years in here. Well, it would have been 15 if I hadn't escaped the day before the trial - with the bed sheets, remember?

Q. But are you sorry for any of this? Do you feel guilty about swindling all those people out of their money?

A. Not really. They were rich, mostly, and they shouldn't have fallen for my scams. Oh, by the way, do you want to buy this gold watch for just five bucks. It's a really rare, top model.

Ooh, let's have a look...

Victor vanishes

What happened next?
- Lustig kept trying to escape from Alcatraz by pretending to be ill.
- Even if he could have got out of the prison, he would have needed a boat to escape the island.
- He became properly ill with pneumonia.
- He was moved to another prison but died there in 1947.

74

Scams, cons and swindles

What else did Victor Lustig get up to in his strange criminal career?

- He dressed in expensive coats and called himself 'Count Lustig'.
- He pretended he owned lots of property, and sold houses that weren't his.
- He tricked banks into lending him money.
- He even tricked the world's most famous GANGSTER, Al Capone, into giving him a thousand dollars!

HOW did he get away with it for so long?

Victor Lustig tricked and fooled people for over 40 years, but how?

- He had good manners, polite charm and a quiet, intelligent approach.
- He also had many disguises in a bag, 47 false names, and loads of fake passports.
- His forged bank notes were very realistic.
- His victims were often too embarrassed to tell anyone, especially the police.

~ An interview with ~
Bonnie
and Clyde

This is a rare interview with two villains at once! I'm in a quiet corner of the Southern USA in the year 1933, and I'm speaking to America's MOST WANTED COUPLE...

Q. Right, so which one is Bonnie and which one's Clyde?
A. What ya talkin' 'bout? Bonnie's a girl's name ain't it? So I'm Clyde and she's Bonnie. Very bonny if yer ask me, hey sweetie?

Q. Ah, right, they're not your surnames, then?
A. Course not! I'm Clyde Barrow and this fine lady is Bonnie Parker.

Q. And who are those three arguing in the car back there?

A. Hey, you do ask a lot of questions, fella. You ain't with the LAW is you? If y'are, we gonna have to shoot you real bad.

Q. No, no, no - do I look like a policeman?

A. No sir, you look like a fancy city fella from somewhere up north. They dress real strange there, so I've heard. If you ain't a cop then why do you want to talk to the Barrow Gang? Ain't you scared we'll rob you?

Q. Yes, but I only have 13p and a broken Doctor Who watch... Anyway, Bonnie, perhaps you'll tell me about the rest of the gang back there in the car. Why *are* they shouting so much?

A. Sure thing, honey. That's Clyde's lazy brother Buck and his whining wife Blanche. The other guy is WD, our buddy. Or he was - we're all fallin' out every day now...

Q. So why are you all falling out?

A. Huh, good question. We're on the run, in case ya didn't know. And if ya didn't, you must be the only guy in America. We're wanted in at least five states - the law been after us for robbery, auto theft and, well, maybe worse now...

Q. Right, er, so are you arguing about what to do? Or maybe who to rob next?

A. We're arguing about EVERYTHING! The police put our pictures in the all the newspapers across the country so everyone's looking out for us. We can't stay in hotels and we can't go home, so we have to sleep cramped up in that dirty old car - and eat out here in woods and fields. I have to wash in freezing cold rivers. I am so FED UP!

Q. I see. Have you got a plan?

A. No we ain't. Ask him - it's his gang.

Q. What are you going to do, Clyde?

A. What *can* I do? Keep running. Maybe get to a state where no one knows us. But we got no money for food or gas, so we have to keep robbing banks and stores.

Q. What's it like, robbing a bank?

A. Terrifying. We get shot at all the time. They usually call the law on us so we have to do it real quick - pulling out guns and showing we ain't afraid to hurt people. Customers are screaming and the bank tellers try and give us just a few dollars so we have to threaten them real fierce, you know? Then we run, dive into the car and hope we don't get a bullet or a chase.

He coulda parked a bit **NEARER!**

Q. Crime doesn't sound to be much fun. Why did you get into it in the first place?

A. Because we was broke! Ain't you heard of the GREAT DEPRESSION?

Q. Well, I've heard of it but... OK what is it?

A. It's going hungry, that's what it is. For years there's been no work, no jobs, no money, no hope. And when you were brought up poor like I was, nobody cares. As a kid we had no home for years – I slept under a wagon with my folks. It makes a man desperate...

Q. What about you, Bonnie?

A. Same. My pa died when I was just four and my ma never had two cents. I ran away when I was fifteen and married some guy. Huh, he turned out useless, ended up in jail. I met Clyde when I was 19. I knew he was a criminal but at least we had fun together... at first.

Q. Is it true your gang has killed police officers and others, Clyde?

A. Listen, I never set out to shoot no one. But some folks, they don't understand danger, y'know? They should just give us what we want and then no one gets hurt. But they is sometimes stupid and so we have to use guns.

Q. You don't HAVE to use them, surely?

A. What do you know, city boy? The cops they're always firing on us! I been hit more than once – and Bonnie too. It's self-defence, that's all.

Q. Right, I, er have decided NOT to argue about that anymore... So, Bonnie, how come your photos are in all the newspapers across the country?

A. Yeah, we were real foolish... We had a hideout and it was a nice little place with somewhere to park the car for getaways too. But the five of us made a lot of noise one night playing cards and someone must have called the cops.

Q. What happened?

A. They waited outside and told us to come out with our hands up. We had to pile in the car and shoot our way out. It all happened so fast. We left behind papers with our names on, and a stolen camera – we'd snapped crazy poses of each other on it. Once the press got hold of those pictures, we were famous... in a BAD way.

Q. You're both still young, only 23 and 24 according to Wikipedia. Is that right?

A. Wiki WHAT? You sure do speak some garbage, fella.

Q. Yeah, I get that a lot. Wikipedia is a, well, it's one of.. it's something that... oh never mind. I was going to say, why not give yourselves up? They might go easy on you because you're young. Clyde?

A. What? WHAT!! I am NOT going back to jail. No way! Anyhow, they'd probably fry us in the ELECTRIC CHAIR for murder now. We gone too far.

Q. Is prison *that* bad?
A. You clearly never been, have you?

Q. I did once get a parking ticket in Giggleswick. But I escape custody for that. Er, why is it so bad?
A. I'll tell you why. They BEAT you, treat you like DIRT every day. And they make you work in the fields all day, like animals. Hard labour they call it. It's BRUTAL. I'd rather risk bullets. It was so bad last time I was in jail I cut off two of my toes so I couldn't walk properly. Got me out of slavin' in the ditches.

Q. That must be why you limp?
A. Correct.

Q. And can I ask you one last question, Clyde?
A. Sure. But I might shoot you. I'm gettin' mighty suspicious now.

Q. Is your middle name really CHESTNUT?
A. Yes. Now where is my rifle?

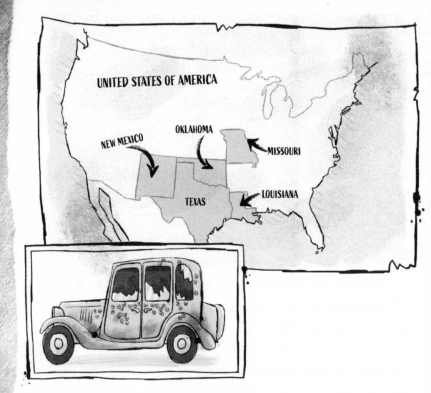

Ambush!

What happened next?

- The gang crashed their car and Bonnie was badly injured.
- Buck was shot by police and Blanche captured.
- A big reward was offered for information about the gang and a special team of agents was formed to track them down.
- In 1934, law officers ambushed their car and shot Bonnie and Clyde dead.

What were the gang's crimes?

In films they may seem like heroes, but in real life the Barrow Gang did terrible things:

- They stole from many ordinary people who were struggling to earn a living.
- They helped a group of convicted criminals to escape from prison.
- They killed nine police officers.
- They murdered at least four other people using guns.

Bad bods

Here are some other famous gangsters in America at the time:

- John Dillinger
- Baby Face Nelson
- Ma Barker
- Pretty Boy Floyd
- Machine Gun Kelly.

John Dillinger

An interview with

Vlad the Impaler

I've now been tranimalated to Transylvania in the year 1475. I am about to meet the person with possibly the WORST reputation in history. Am I scared? YES.

Q. You keeping well, Mr Impaler?
A. Not really, no.

Q. So, er, what's the problem? Not been getting enough impaling action recently?
A. My guard tells me you're a historian from the West. He said you want to hear my side of events in Romania, to put them down in writing. There are just two problems. One, I have never heard of Romania, and two, you look like a trickster.

Q. But we're in Romania, according to my machine - I thought that's where you live. Oh, and I promise no tricks.

A. Well, this is Transylvania, not my homeland.

Q. Oh. Where is your homeland?

A. Wallachia, to the south of course! I am Vlad III, true ruler of that territory.

Q. So, why are you here?

A. Because my NINCOMPOOPER of a brother Radu has taken it over, with the help of the Turks. Their Ottoman Empire has ruined my life!

Q. Oh dear, what are you going to do?

A. I am making appeals to the Hungarians and the Moldavians. With their help I can be restored as ruler of Wallachia for the third time! Then we must defeat the Ottoman threat...

Q. Wow, it's all very, er *complicated*... Can I ask, why are you called 'The Impaler'?

A. It's a family tradition thing - we're all called 'the something'. My dad was Vlad the Dragon, my horrid younger brother is Radu the Handsome and I also have a relation called Vlad the Monk.

Radu the Handsome

Vlad the Dragon

Vlad the Monk

Q. Ah, so your brother is REALLY annoying. Most annoying brothers just burp a lot and pinch your crisps but yours has stolen your kingdom and he's really good-looking while you're just, er... *ooh, I probably shouldn't have started this sentence...*

A. Just WHAT?

Q. Good at impaling? What is impaling anyway?

A. It's skewering. I have my enemies gored on big wooden stakes. It's my favourite form of execution - sends out a very clear message. DON'T MESS WITH ME.

Q. I can see that, yes. But isn't it just a bit, well, cruel? Nasty? Vicious? Evil? Barbarous?

A. Indeed. That's why it works. It's a deterrent. When Sultan Mehmed II invaded my lands in 1462 with a vast army of 90,000 Turks, he met a whole forest of my victims, impaled on sharpened poles - thousands of them. The soldiers turned around, quaking in their boots, ha!

Q. So, why *are* you so, erm, keen on the whole KILLING thing?

A. You are supposed to be a man who knows history! You must be aware of what has been done to me! I have been orphaned, betrayed, pursued by enemies and forced into exile. And that's just for starters... GAH. I seek only revenge. And total loyalty. And obedience. Death is a compelling lesson for those who disagree...

Q. Have you ever considered an anger management course?

A. What?

Q. I was thinking, maybe you could work out your rage in the gym rather than spiking people like barbecue sausages. I've got a discount voucher somewhere.

A. Enough babbling! I think that perhaps it is time for another impaling...

Q. Hang on a sec, before you stick me on a stick, I have one more question. It's the one all my readers will want to know.

A. Very well, a final question. Like your final meal. What is it?

Q. Are you a vampire?

A. A what?

Q. You know, a bloodsucker, a member of the undead, the Prince of Darkness and all that?

A. What are you talking about?

Q. Wait a sec, I'd better get some garlic just in case... Drat, I left it in 1759. Right, it's just that there's a book and a load of films called *Dracula*, and some people say you're him. Is it true?

A. Ah, my father was Vlad Dracula, indeed, and I sometimes use that title too.

Q. Yikes! It's TRUE. Can I borrow some silver bullets, a cross and a wooden stake please?

A. I have plenty of stakes...

Q. If you bite me in the neck, my publishers will be REALLY CROSS. I've got more books to do! Actually, your teeth are quite blunt. Where's your cape? And that comedy moustache is going to get *caked* in blood. I... I don't think you're a vampire at all. Are you?

A. Enough of your yammering. Guards, bring my deluxe impaling kit, the one my auntie got me for Christmas.

Q. I'm going now. It's been horrible meeting you.

A. Wait, I need to skewer somebody... POO, he's gone.

Bad for Vlad

What happened next?

- Vlad wanted to become ruler of Wallachia again so he gathered an army.
- He was opposed by the Ottoman Turks, plus local people who hated his cruelty.
- After two battles, Vlad was eventually captured by his enemies.
- They cut off his head and that was that - no more impaling!

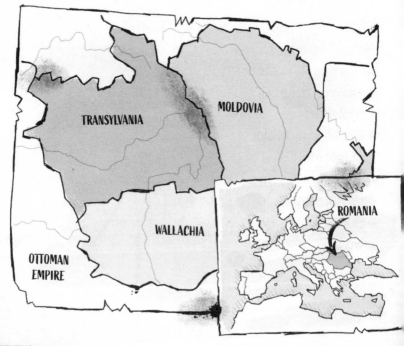

The Dracula thing...

Some people still believe that Vlad the Impaler
was the real Dracula - why?

- In 1897 a writer called Bram Stoker wrote his
  famous novel *Dracula* about a vampire.
- The story was set in Transylvania after Stoker
  read a book about its history.
- He learned about the real Vlad Dracula, the
  Drac part of the name means 'dragon' or 'devil'.
- He used the name for his fictional vampire, and
  the book went on be a worldwide bestseller...

Was he REALLY that nasty?

Historians think Vlad was a cruel ruler but it's hard to
be sure of the details:

- He lived over 500 years ago and reliable evidence is
  tricky to find.
- Old history books are not always trustworthy sources
  of information.
- There are medieval books which describe Vlad doing
  terrible things to his victims BUT...
- Some of these were written by his enemies, so can
  we believe them?

An interview with

Zheng Yi Sao

My trusty tranimalator has time-travelled me to the South China Sea now, in the year 1809, to meet history's most powerful female pirate. I'm SCARED!

Q. Er, hello Zheng. Is it OK if I call you that?

A. Where did YOU come from? Who are you and how did you get onto my junk?

Q. Oh, I wouldn't call this a pile of junk - it's quite a nice big sailing ship really, isn't it?

A. FOOL! This type of vessel is called a junk. Now answer my questions or I will slice you up myself.

Q. *Gulp, I thought I was asking the questions...* It's kind of hard to explain, really. I'm from Britain and I want to find out all about what you're doing, is that alright?

A. Aha! I thought you looked like an Englishman. And you even admit you are spying on us! Do you want to DIE? You are certainly asking for it!

Q. Whoops. You don't like Britain?

A. They are my enemy! Along with the Chinese rulers and the interfering Portuguese, they are gathering ships to fight us and put an end to our domination of these seas. But you must know this already!

Q. Nope, I don't know anything about you really. Can't I just ask a few teeny harmless questions?

A. Men, kill him!

Q. Oi! Watch where you're putting that cutlass! Ouch, that hurt! OI, YOU'VE CHOPPED MY ARM OFF! That was one of my best arms... and now I'm bleeding all over my shoes... I'm a goner... goodbye world... WAIT, I can go back in time with the tranimalator and NOT BE DEAD! Here goes...

A. UHH! What happened, he JUST DISAPPEARED! It must be some fiendish spy trick. Search the ship, now!

An hour before

Q. *Yesss, two arms again!* Er, hello, mighty Zheng! I am, erm, a fellow pirate who wishes to, ah, join your crew. And I'm definitely not British. Are you interested?

A. How did you get aboard? Where's your boat? And you don't LOOK like a pirate to me. You sound quite BRITISH too...

Q. Oh no, no, no, I just went there on holiday once and, er, picked up the accent. Easily done. Anyway, I see you are a mighty and powerful pirate leader, Zheng. Are all these ships - I mean junks - yours?

A. Of course. I am the commander of 226 pirate vessels and 17,000 crew! We rule these seas, everyone knows that. Along with my second in command, Zhang Bao, I lead five fleets with a strict code of conduct under coloured flags: red, white, blue, yellow and purple. We did have six until a few weeks ago, gah!

Q. What happened?

A. The Black Flag Fleet are traitors! They turned against us and surrendered to the Chinese Navy - our ENEMIES! And now warships from England and Portugal are joining them. They want to stop our raids and plundering.

Q. I've always wondered how you plunder. So, what kind of, er, raids do you do? Any good ones?

A. Yes! We surround any ship we want and take their cargoes. It has made us rich! And since my husband died, I have brought all the fleets together and now we are powerful enough to steal from the towns along the coast of China too.

Q. What happened to your husband?

A. He was a mighty pirate, but he fell overboard in a storm. Very sad.

Q. You don't look very sad. Are you?

A. Well, alright, his loss did allow me to take over and create the mightiest pirate force in the world, so it was kind of handy...

Q. Does it ever occur to you that all the killing and stealing you do is WRONG?

A. No.

Q. Well, it might be, don't you think?

A. Possibly. I don't like killing people really. I'm sure it hurts.

Q. It does, A LOT! Erm, I would imagine... Anyway, what if you're captured by one of these enemy ships with big cannons?

A. That's a good point. They might torture me. Perhaps I should give up while I'm at the top. Maybe take up the oboe instead. Yes, you've convinced me.

Q. Wait! NO. You can't.

A. What, why not?

Q. In all the time-travelly books I've read, it's BAD for a person from the future to go back and change the past. It messes with MASSIVE FORCES and can have DISASTROUS CONSEQUENCES. If you become an oboe player then WHO KNOWS WHAT COULD HAPPEN? And it would be my fault.

A. I didn't understand any of that.

Q. I think you should carry on being a pirate. You're BRILLIANT at it. I mean, look at all these junks you command! You won't stop, will you? TERRIBLE THINGS could be unleashed...

A. You know what? I am thinking you are just trouble. Or a complete TWIT. Perhaps I should kill you. Men!

Q. NO! Don't, my cat will miss me.

A. Oh alright, but I'm definitely stopping the pirate thing and learning the oboe.

Q. No, don't! *I know, I'll use the tranimalator to go back in time again.* See ya sooner!

A: WHAT! He just VANISHED! Where did he go? Search the ship everyone!

The day before

Q. Y*essss, back again!* Er, hello mighty Zheng. I have come here from the Black Flag Fleet to say they're really sorry and were wrong to surrender and that you're the BEST PIRATE LEADER in the GALAXY and that you should carry on and never touch an oboe. Is that OK?

A. Who is this clown? Men, kill him!

NOT AGAIN! Owww, that's really sore! And don't cut that off, I need it! Tranimalator, save me...

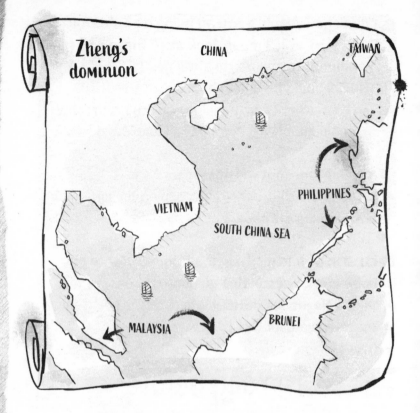

Buccaneers busted

What happened next?

- The Black Flag Fleet joined with the Chinese Navy against Zheng's forces.
- With Britain and Portugal also against her, Zheng decided to give up piracy.
- She did a deal and agreed to surrender her 226 ships if she was pardoned (forgiven).
- Zheng lived a peaceful life as a rich retired brigand.

Was her pirate fleet really that big?

Written records show that Zheng not only had 226 ships...

- She led a force of 17,318 pirates – that's a LOT of 'yarrr-ing'!
- Her ships were armed with a total of 1,315 cannons.
- When she surrendered, Zheng was aged just 35.

Fearsome tactics

Chinese pirates of the 1800s terrified the crews of ships using these devices:

- Grappling hooks
- Knives on long poles
- Fireships
- Small bombs.

~ An interview with ~
Billy the Kid

I'm now in jail again! Well, not me really - I'm here to interview celebrated cowboy and outlaw Billy the Kid, in the year 1881 in New Mexico, USA. He's the one in jail...

Q. Is your name really Billy the Kid?

A. No, that's what the newspapers call me! I'm William H. Bonney.

Q. But I thought your name was Henry McCarty. Erm, isn't it?

A. Well, yes, no point pretending no more now I'm sentenced to hang. I was called Henry as a kid, true. I guess I'm still a kid, being only 21.

Q. So, why not Henry the Kid?

A. There was people wanted to kill me, that's why. Here in New Mexico and in Arizona. I was blamed for crimes I didn't do. They came after me and I've been on the run for years, so I changed my name - you know, to try and conceal my identity.

Q. If you're innocent then why are you in prison, condemned to die?

A. Good question. They say I'm guilty but I ain't. They said I killed Sheriff Brady but it wasn't me. There was a gun battle and plenty of people was shootin' on both sides. Sure, Brady took a bullet, but they can't prove it was mine. He was trying to kill me anyway, so my firing was self-defence, you know?

Q. But what about the other men you killed at other times?

A. This is a dangerous place, sir. That's why they call it the Wild West. There's gunslingers out here and outlaws and fearful Apaches, and the law ain't fair to men like me. Listen, you gotta help me escape!

Q. Me? Erm, I don't think I'd be very good at that – I have trouble getting out of bed, never mind prison cells. Have you got a plan?

A. No, but you got in here somehow, din't ya? I reckon that machine there has something to do with it. If you help me escape, I'll make it worth your while.

Q. And what if I don't?

A. Then you, sir, will be my final victim...

Q. *Gulp.* Ooh, well, here's an idea. You tell me your story and I'll see what I can do with the tranimalator, OK?

A. It's a deal. What d'you want to know?

I only came into town for bubblegum!

Q. First, what was your childhood like?

A. Phewf, it was tough. I was born and raised in big old New York City. My pa died when I was young and ma took us off around the states tryin' to settle. But she took ill and passed away when I was 15. It was tough, you know, being an orphan.

Q. What happened to you?

A. I had a rented room in a house in Silver City and I got a job, but I was always hungry. I stole food and clothes and then I got caught and put in jail. But I escaped. I was a fugitive then, at just 16 years old.

Q. So you were on the run from the Law. Where did you go?

A. I had to get away from New Mexico where I was wanted. I went to Arizona and worked on a ranch as a cattle hand.

Q. You were a cowboy?

A. Yeah, a really bad one. Lost all my wages gambling too. I met this no-good fella, Mackie his name was. We started stealing horses and I was in trouble again.

Q. How did all the shooting and killing happen?

A. Everyone round here has a gun. It's the way of life. I got into a fight with this hateful blacksmith one day and I thought he was gonna kill me, so I shot him and ran. I guess he died.

Q. It's VERY violent here in nineteenth century America. Can't you just settle arguments with a game of rock, paper, scissors instead?

A. You sure talk some tosh, sir.

Q. That's what most of my school reports said... Anyway, what happened to you next?

A. Whoah, all sorts. I joined a band of cattle rustlers and then I got caught up in the Lincoln County War. That's when my troubles really started...

Q. A WAR? Were you a soldier?

A. No, it was a stupid series of gun battles between two feuding ranch owners over money and land. It's a long story but I ended up in a big gun fight and Sheriff Brady on the other side got shot and I got blamed. That's why I'm here in this jail, awaiting execution. It's unfair.

Q. What did the judge say in court?

A. Huh! He was SURE glad to have me on trial! The evidence was weak but he said I was guilty and will 'hang until you are DEAD, DEAD, DEAD'.

Q. Yikes. What did you say?

A. Told him he could go to HELL, HELL, HELL. It kept the reporters happy anyway.

Q. So how did you get captured in the end?

A. Well, after Brady died the Governor put out a $500 reward for my capture. That's a mighty motivation for a hungry man...

Q. Wow that's equal to HUNDREDS OF THOUSANDS today. I might go back in time, catch you and claim it myself! *Ooh, pretend you didn't hear that.* Erm, who was it that caught you?

A. Good old Sheriff Pat Garrett, that's who. Came after me with a posse.

Q. He chased you with a CAT?

A. A POSSE not a PUSSY!

Q. Oops, my bad. So, that's why you're here in chains?

A. Sure is. He ambushed me at Stinking Springs. A bad smell and a bad memory...

Q. Right, thank you, Mr Kid. I mean, William. I mean Henry. I've, er, got to go now.

A. Not so fast - you said you'd help me escape!

Q. Oh yes, sorry. I'll just, erm, set the tranimalator to BREAKOUT mode...

A. Good. You wouldn't trick a man on death row, would y- HEY, WHERE'S HE GONE?

Billy busts out

What happened next?

- While in jail waiting to be hanged, Billy asked to go to the outdoor toilet.
- Billy used his handcuffs to hit the deputy sheriff taking him.
- He then shot the officer and escaped, cutting his chains with an axe.
- After three months on the run, Billy was found and shot dead by Sheriff Pat Garrett.

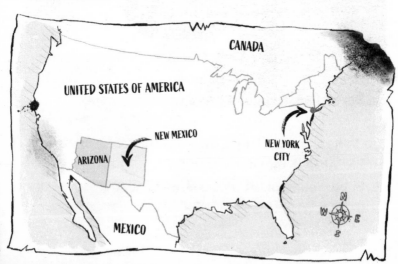

CANADA

UNITED STATES OF AMERICA

NEW MEXICO

ARIZONA

NEW YORK CITY

MEXICO

Strange rumours...

Some people claimed that it was not actually Billy the Kid who was shot by the sheriff in 1881:

- It was dark when the shooting happened.
- The body was buried but many people said it wasn't really him.
- Several men later claimed to be the real Henry McCarty/William Bonney/Billy the Kid.
- The case is still disputed to this day!

Billy the Star

The true story of Billy the Kid has been told in LOTS of ways:

- Over 50 films
- Loads of books
- Several plays
- Multiple songs
- TV shows
- Video games.

An interview with

Quiz

Q 1. What was Blackbeard's real name?

a. Bluebeard ☐
b. Bigbeard ☐
c. Edward Teach ☐
d. Edgar Torch ☐

Q 2. Which of these things did Blackbeard capture from other ships in the Caribbean Sea?

a. Cocoa ☐   b. Toast ☐
c. Cheese ☐   d. Lemonade ☐

Q 3. What was Guy Fawkes trying to blow up when he was arrested?

a. A balloon ☐   b. The Houses of Parliament ☐
c. King Charles I ☐   d. The Tower of London ☐

Q 4. What gave away the Gunpowder Plot?

a. A priest ☐   b. An undercover agent ☐
c. A letter ☐   d. A big TV investigation ☐

Q 5. Nero was emperor in which city?

a. Tokyo ☐ b. Preston ☐

c. Rome ☐ d. Gotham City ☐

Q 6. As well as poisoning people, Nero liked to do what?

a. Poetry ☐ b. Knitting ☐

c. DIY ☐ d. Basketball ☐

Q 7. Why did outlaw Ned Kelly's dad get transported to Australia?

a. He kidnapped two donkeys ☐

b. He stole two pigs ☐

c. He panicked two squid ☐

d. He ate too much ☐

Q 8. Who got a 56-page letter from Ned Kelly?

a. The police ☐

b. The Beatles ☐

c. The Prime Minister ☐

d. The Kelly Gang ☐

Q 9. What did Ivan the Terrible make the Archbishop of Novgorod do?

a. Moonwalking ☐

b. Pray for 40 days without food ☐

c. Dress like a penguin ☐

d. Marry a horse ☐

Q 10. How old was Ivan the Terrible when he became ruler of Russia?

a. 16 ☐   b. 3 ☐

c. 49 ☐   d. 328 ☐

Q 11. What did Victor Lustig sell to a scrap metal dealer in Paris?

a. Fake coins ☐   b. His granny ☐

c. A bronze statue ☐   d. The Eiffel Tower ☐

Q 12. Victor Lustig made a device to print fake banknotes. What was it called?

a. The Bulgarian Chest ☐   b. The Turkish Tin ☐

c. The Rumanian Box ☐   d. Wendy ☐

Q 13. How did the police know what US gangsters Bonnie and Clyde looked like?

a. They left behind photos of themselves ☐

b. They forced an artist to paint their portraits ☐

c. They sent a description to the newspapers ☐

d. They were caught on CCTV in a bank ☐

Q 14. How did the police stop Bonnie and Clyde in the end?

a. By ambush ☐

b. By asking them nicely ☐

c. By tracking them with dogs ☐

d. By sheer luck ☐

Q 15. Vlad the Impaler was king of where?

a. Romania ☐   b. Transylvania ☐

c. Moldovia ☐   d. Wallachia ☐

Q 16. Which fictional baddie was inspired by Vlad the Impaler?

a. Frankenstein ☐   b. Dracula ☐

c. Darth Vader ☐   d. Impaler Man ☐

Q 17. Which of these crimes did Billy the Kid not commit?

a. Horse stealing ☐   b. Cattle rustling ☐

c. Murder ☐   d. Stealing a lawnmower ☐

Q 18. Where did sheriff Pat Garrett capture Billy the Kid?

a. Smelly Streams ☐   b. Pongy Ponds ☐

c. Stinking Springs ☐   d. Eggy Everglades ☐

Q 19. The Chinese Pirate Zheng Yi Sao sailed what kind of boat?

a. A bunk ☐   b. A hunk ☐

c. A junk ☐   d. A punk ☐

Q 20. How many pirates did Zheng command?

a. 17 ☐   b. 170 ☐

c. 1,700 ☐   d. 17,000 ☐

Glossary

ambush To make a surprise attack on someone from a hidden position.

Apache A member of a Native American tribe living mainly in the southwestern part of the United States of America.

binnacle A case that holds and protects a ship's compass. It is located near the helm of the ship.

blockade To seal off or block a place to prevent people or goods entering or leaving.

Boudica (around 30 CE–60 or 61 CE) Ancient British queen of the Iceni. She led a revolt against Roman rule in Britain in 60 CE.

brigand A person (or member of a gang) that attacks other people and steals from them.

British Empire All the places around the world that were once ruled by Britain.

buccaneer A pirate; any of the pirates or government sponsored adventurers who raided the Spanish colonies and the ships sailing in the Caribbean Sea in the 17th and 18th centuries.

bushranger Any of the bandits of the Australian bush or outback, who robbed or attacked the settlers and Aborigines of the Australian frontier in the late 18th and early 19th centuries. They specialised in robbing stagecoaches, banks and small settlements.

Catholic A member of the Catholic Church and a follower of the Christian religion. The word itself means 'universal'.

Claudius (10 BCE–54 CE) The fourth Roman emperor from 41 CE to 54 CE. He was succeeded by Nero, his grand-nephew and legally adopted stepson.

counterfeit A fraudulent (false) imitation of something else.

cringle A loop at the corner of a sail to which a rope is attached.

emperor A ruler of an empire.

George I (1660–1727) First Hanoverian king of Great Britain from 1714 to 1727.

high treason The crime of betraying one's country, especially by trying to kill or overthrow the government or sovereign.

House of Lords One of the two parts of the UK parliament. Its members are not elected by voters.

Houses of Parliament The buildings where the British parliament does its work.

King James VI and I (1566–1625) King of Scotland as James VI from 1567 to 1625 and first Stuart king of England from 1603 to 1625.

landlubber Someone who has little knowledge of boats or the sea and is not used to travelling by boat.

loot To steal goods or private property from a place or person, typically during a war.

lyre A stringed instrument, used especially in ancient Greece.

mizzen The mast or tall pole that supports the sails in front of a ship's main mast.

Mount Olympus In Greek mythology the mountain where the gods lived.

Ottoman Empire Founded in about 1300, a former Islamic-run Turkish empire that ruled large areas of Eastern Europe, North Africa and the Middle East for more than 600 years until 1922.

poop deck A short deck that forms the roof of a cabin located at the back (aft) of a ship.

privateer A person or an armed ship authorised by a government to attack and steal from ships at sea, especially in the 17th and 18th centuries.

Protestant A follower of the Christian religion who belongs to the branch of the Christian Church which separated from the Catholic Church in the 16th century.

Queen Anne (1665-1714) Queen of Great Britain and Ireland from 1702 to 1714.

Queen Elizabeth I (1533-1603) Queen of England and Ireland from 1558 to 1603.

scurvy A disease caused by a deficiency of vitamin C. Until the end of the 18th century, undernourished sailors were particularly affected by this disease.

Senate The governing and advisory assembly in the ancient Roman Republic, made up of the aristocracy.

skipper The captain of a ship.

sloop A small sailing boat with one mast.

State Opening of Parliament A ceremonial event that marks the start of a parliamentary year and sets out the government's agenda for that year.

Sultan Mehmed II (1432-1481) Sultan of the Ottoman Empire from 1444 to 1446 and from 1451 to 1481.

The Great Depression A period of severe worldwide economic decline with widespread unemployment, which began in 1929 and lasted throughout the 1930s.

tsar The male Russian ruler or emperor (until the 1917 revolution).

Index

Have you read...

Interview with **Cleopatra** & Other Famous Rulers

Written by **Andy Seed**

Illustrated by **Gareth Conway**

Turn the page for a sneak peek of Andy's interview with one of the most famous rulers of the ancient world.

~ An interview with ~
Cleopatra

For this interview, I travel back to the year 32BCE, to Ancient Egypt, to meet possibly the most famous queen that ever lived...

Q. Hello, er, Your Majesty, it's very good of you to meet me. This is exciting - I've never chatted to a pharaoh before.

A. I have met many strange people in my time but nothing as strange as you.

Q. That's because I am from the future!

A. So my advisers tell me... quite a claim. Well, we rulers are always eager to discover what tomorrow brings.

Q. Ah, you want to know the weather forecast? Hang on while I just open the app...

A. What is that curious object? Some kind of divining stone? An amulet?

Q. No, just my old smartphone.

A. A what?

Q. Er, it's a device for, well, ooh, this is going to be quite tricky to explain... Oh, no WiFi. Well, I suppose it is 32BCE and we are in the desert...

A. Stranger, what exactly do you want?

Q. May I just ask you a few questions? It won't take long.

A. Hmmm, very well. But if I think you're a Roman spy I will have my soldiers cut you into dog food.

Q. Fair enough, gulp. So, er, what was your childhood like?

A. I was born and brought up here in the Royal Palace in Alexandria. My father was Ptolemy XII, Pharaoh, so my childhood was not exactly ordinary.

Q. It's a very grand building, lots of bling.

A. Of course, it must be suitable for rulers of the mighty Kingdom of Egypt. And now it is **mine**.